THE MISINFORMATION MAZE

A TALE OF FAMILY, FACTS, AND FICTION

RANJEET SINGH

Made with ♥ on the Notion Press Platform
www.notionpress.com

This book is dedicated to the sacred memory of my beloved father, Late Ghanshyam Singh. A man of few words but infinite wisdom, he was not just a father but also a mentor and beacon of light that guided me through the labyrinth of life. A steadfast educator, he wore the mantle of a School Principal for over fifteen years, touching and moulding innumerable lives with his profound knowledge and nurturing spirit.

His influence extended far beyond the confines of our home, reaching the corners of classrooms, igniting young minds, and fostering a love for learning. His wisdom was not limited to academic pursuits; it was a compass that helped navigate the complex terrains of life. His teachings were not just lessons but timeless values we carry in our hearts.

His departure in 2012 left an irreplaceable void in our lives. Yet, his spirit continues to live on - in every word we write, every lesson we learn, every stride we take. His indelible mark is evident in every endeavour we undertake. Like an eternal flame, his teachings continue to guide us even in his physical absence.

This book is a small tribute to his towering persona, a humble effort to keep his legacy alive. Here's to my father, my guide, my inspiration - your teachings continue to be our guiding star.

Contents

Foreword

In an era where information is at our fingertips, it is simultaneously a blessing and a curse. The gift is the real-time access to information from all corners of the globe. The curse is the overwhelming abundance of it, often leading to the spread of Misinformation. 'The Misinformation Maze: A Tale of Family, Facts, and Fiction' is a book that bravely delves into this paradox.

In a landscape saturated with quick-fix solutions and instant gratification, this book stands out as a beacon of truth and a guide to the conscious consumption of information. Through the journey of the Kulkarni family, readers are subtly yet powerfully guided to question, explore, and understand the world of Misinformation.

The author, with great sensitivity, explores the dynamics of a family grappling with the chaos of Misinformation. Each character adds a unique perspective, revealing how Misinformation is not just a social issue but a personal one, impacting our daily lives and decisions.

In this engaging narrative, the author successfully demystifies complex concepts like cognitive biases, echo chambers, and the Dunning-Kruger effect, making them accessible to everyone. The book's true power lies in exploring these concepts and the solutions it provides.

As you turn the pages of this book, you will witness the transformative journey of a family and, hopefully, embark on your own. The book's real triumph lies in its potential to spark a change - in how we consume, share, and interact with the information surrounding us.

As we step into an increasingly digital future, 'The Misinformation Maze: A Tale of Family, Facts, and Fiction' is a compass that points us towards responsible information consumption. It is a call to action for us to become more conscious, discerning, and accountable in the face of the information avalanche.

So, dear reader, as you prepare to dive into the world of the Kulkarni family, I invite you to challenge your preconceptions, question the information you consume, and, most importantly, enjoy the ride through 'The Misinformation Maze.'

Happy reading!

Preface

We are all on a relentless quest for truth in the information age. Amidst the ceaseless tide of data that floods our screens daily, sifting facts from fiction has become an imperative skill. ‘The Misinformation Maze: A Tale of Family, Facts, and Fiction’ was conceived to tackle this challenge.

When I first contemplated writing this book, my goal was not just to educate but to engage, not just to inform, but to inspire. I wanted to create a narrative that unravelled the complexities of Misinformation, cognitive biases, and echo chambers in a relatable and accessible way. The Kulkarni family was born out of this desire - a mirror to every family navigating the labyrinth of information and Misinformation in their daily lives.

As I penned down their journey, I found myself confronting my biases, questioning my sources of information, and learning along with them. The trip was as enlightening as I hope it will be for you.
This book is not just a story about a family’s struggle and triumphs over Misinformation; it’s a plea for critical thinking, a tribute to truth, and a call to action for every reader. It encourages us to question, verify, and hold ourselves accountable for the information we share and consume.

As you delve into the pages of this book, I invite you to journey alongside the Kulkarnis, witness their struggles and victories, learn from their insights, and reflect on your

relationship with information.
I hope that 'The Misinformation Maze: A Tale of Family, Facts, and Fiction' serves as a beacon, guiding you towards a more conscious, discerning, and responsible consumption of information. It is a small step towards battling the behemoth of Misinformation that threatens to engulf us.

Ultimately, the journey through the misinformation maze is not a sprint but a marathon. It's not a battle to be won overnight, but a continuous commitment to truth, learning, and growth. This book serves as a stepping stone to discerning the validity.

With hope and curiosity,
Ranjeet Singh

Acknowledgements

Writing a book is a journey one rarely takes alone, and 'The Misinformation Maze: A Tale of Family, Facts, and Fiction' is no exception. I am deeply indebted to many individuals whose support and encouragement have been invaluable.

First and foremost, I would like to express my profound gratitude to my family. Your unwavering belief in my capabilities, your patience during my long hours of writing, and your invaluable feedback have been instrumental in shaping this book. Thank you for being my sounding board, critics, and cheerleaders.

I extend my heartfelt thanks to my colleagues at work for your understanding and flexibility during this process. Your camaraderie and encouragement, particularly during challenging times, have been a source of strength.

My sincere thanks to my editor, whose keen eye and astute suggestions have immensely enhanced the readability and coherence of this book. Your expertise and dedication are much appreciated.

Lastly, I would like to express my gratitude to the readers. Your interest and engagement are the reason I am writing. This book contributes meaningfully to your understanding of Misinformation. It equips you with the tools to navigate today's complex information landscape.

Thank you all for being a part of this journey.

Prologue

In the digital era, information is at our fingertips. We are exposed to a world of News, stories, and ideas with a click, a swipe, and a quick scroll. But the line between fact and fiction often blurs in this vast digital landscape.

Welcome to "The Misinformation Maze: A Tale of Family, Facts, and Fiction."

This book, set in the vibrant city of Jabalpur in India, presents a tale of a typical family navigating the complex world of social media and Misinformation. It explores how digital habits impact our lives, relationships, and perception of reality. It is a story that could happen in any home, anywhere in the world.

Our protagonists are the Kulkarnis - Vijay, a businessman; Sangeeta, a school teacher; and their children, Vikrant and Sulochana. Like many of us, this family is plugged into the digital world. They consume, create, and share content, unaware of the potential repercussions. But when a single post sparks a storm of controversy, they find themselves in the throes of the misinformation maze.

As we delve deeper into this digital age, we are continually reminded of the implications of our online actions. Our every post, share, and like can have repercussions beyond our screens. Navigating this world is not unlike journeying through a dense jungle, where each step can either lead us towards the truth or draw us deeper into the undergrowth of Misinformation.

In this book, you will journey with the Kulkarnis as they traverse this digital wilderness. You will watch as they confront their misconceptions, challenge their long-held beliefs, and learn to question the information they consume. You will discover that this tale is not just about a family in Jabalpur but about all of us who are part of this interconnected digital ecosystem.

"The Misinformation Maze: A Tale of Family, Facts, and Fiction" explores our collective online behaviour. It delves into how we, as a society, often unknowingly contribute to the spread of Misinformation. It exposes the dangerous echo chambers we inadvertently create and highlights the urgent need for digital literacy.

But beyond the cautionary tale, this book is also a story of hope. It demonstrates that while the digital world can be a breeding ground for Misinformation, it also holds the key to combating it. It shows that each one of us has the power to stem the tide of Misinformation and, in doing so, create a more informed, more responsible digital community.

With the help of their friends and experts, the Kulkarnis embark on a journey to understand, navigate, and counter the spread of Misinformation. They learn about the importance of fact-checking, responsible sharing power, and unverified News's impact.

This book is a reflection of our times. It highlights the challenges we face in the era of information overload and our responsibility as consumers and creators of digital content. It's a tale that will make you question, make you think, and hopefully, make you act.

You will be drawn into the Kulkarnis' journey, struggles, victories, and lessons as you turn the pages. You will witness the power of Misinformation and the strength of truth. You will see the world through their eyes, and you will see a reflection of your own digital habits.

So, as you embark on this journey with the Kulkarnis, prepare to navigate the intricate paths of the misinformation maze. It might be challenging and unsettling, but it will be enlightening. And remember, every step you take, every page you turn, is a step towards a more informed, more responsible digital world.

So, are you ready to step into the maze?

CHAPTER ONE

The Digital Breakfast

The sun had barely risen over the bustling city of Jabalpur when the Kulkarni household was already abuzz with activity. A heated debate, typically reserved for the evening news, had erupted at the breakfast table. Vijay Kulkarni, a respected businessman with an imposing presence, had just shared a controversial news piece on their family group.

"But Vijay," his wife Sangeeta argued, "how can you blindly trust these social media posts? Don't you remember the last time when..."

Before she could finish, their son Vikrant interjected, his teenage voice breaking with intensity, "She's right, Papa. You can't just share something without verifying it first."

Vijay stubbornly waved them off, "I know what I'm doing. And people must know about this."

This was not an unfamiliar scene in the Kulkarni household, a compact yet cosy home in the heart of Jabalpur, a small city with a unique blend of urban modernity and traditional charm. The town, known for its vibrant markets, historic landmarks, and friendly people, mirrored the Kulkarnis in many ways - modern yet rooted in traditional values.

Much like their city, their house blended old and new. The walls are adorned with black and white family portraits alongside colourful modern art, the shelves filled with worn-out classics and the latest bestsellers, and the living room features an old radio set and a new flat-screen TV. This home was a testament to the family's ethos – respecting tradition while embracing the new.

Vijay, a second-generation businessman, had built a reputable position in the city's textile industry. Sangeeta, a respected school teacher, was known for her balanced views and thoughtfulness. Their 15-year-old son, Vikrant, was a bright student who dreamed of becoming a Youtube gaming influencer. The youngest member, Sulochana, was a lively 10-year-old with many hobbies that changed with the seasons.

In this bustling household, social media was as much a part of their routine as their morning cup of tea. But that morning, as they delved deeper into their digital habits over breakfast, they were oblivious to how their lives would change.

As Vijay left for work and Sangeeta and the kids got ready for their day, they were unaware of the controversy that was about to unfurl from the news piece shared by Vijay. The family found themselves in the eye of a digital storm, their actions having far-reaching consequences they had never anticipated.
The day moved in its usual rhythm, the bustling city of

Jabalpur offering a colourful backdrop to the unfolding story. At the Kulkarni household, the morning's exchange was still remembered. Sangeeta, finishing her school work, decided to call her friend, Priya, a fellow teacher and someone she often turned to for advice.

"Sangeeta, you need to talk to Vijay," Priya suggested after hearing about the morning's incident. "This is not the first time, and you know how quickly these things can spiral out of control."

A few kilometres away, ensconced within his corporate office's glass and steel edifice, Vijay found himself in the eye of a storm he hadn't seen coming. The usually bustling open floor plan, with its air of camaraderie and productivity, was now drowned out by the incessant buzz of his phone. The room, bathed in the harsh glow of fluorescent lights, felt far too bright and loud.

His workstation, a neat and organized island amidst the sea of desks, was now a stage for an unexpected confrontation. His phone, usually a benign companion, was now an incessant adversary. Notifications rolled in like waves crashing against a rocky shore, each ping another message, another comment, another reaction to the post he had shared.

The virtual debate had spilt over into his physical reality, the lines between the digital world and his workspace blurring. Friends and colleagues, familiar faces he shared laughs and coffee breaks with, were now part of the polarized audience. Some were appreciative, thanking him for his bravery in sharing what they deemed vital information. Their messages of support are punctuated with thumbs-up emojis and words of encouragement.

However, not all were in agreement. An equal number, if not more, were critical. They accused him of being reckless, spreading unverified claims, and inciting panic. These messages were laced with disappointment and a hint of betrayal. Their words stung, carving deep grooves of regret into his conscience.

Vijay felt a knot of anxiety twist in his gut. He had merely intended to inform, to help. He hadn't anticipated this backlash, this division. His mind whirled, thoughts tumbling over each other. The usually vibrant office environment now felt stifling, the chatter and clatter a discordant symphony to his predicament. He had unintentionally stepped into a quagmire of Misinformation, and now, he had to find a way out.

Meanwhile, Vikrant sat in his room, engrossed in his game. However, his mind was elsewhere, replaying the morning's conversation. He decided to text his online friend, Arjun, who had a knack for finding the truth behind these viral news stories. "Hey, Arjun, can you check this out?" he typed, sharing the controversial article.

Nestled within the comfortable familiarity of their home, young Sulochana found herself adrift in a sea of adult worries she couldn't quite comprehend. At ten, her universe revolved around simpler things - school, friends, and her beloved books. Yet, she couldn't ignore the peculiar undercurrent that had taken hold of her home.

The four walls of their abode, usually resonating with light-hearted chatter and laughter, now echoed with a tense silence occasionally punctuated by hushed whispers. Even though she couldn't fully grasp the intricacies of the term 'misinformation', its effects on her family were all too apparent.

Her parents, usually the pillars of serenity and assurance, now shared worried glances that they thought were beyond her understanding. Their once relaxed faces were now etched with lines of concern, their voices carrying an unfamiliar note of anxiety. Hushed phone conversations, filled with words too big and concepts too complex for Sulochana, were now a common occurrence.

Sulochana felt the shift in the house's atmosphere, the tension as palpable as the humid summer air outside. The cheerful banter that typically filled their meals was replaced by a stifling quiet, their usually lively living room now a stage for silent contemplation. Gone were the playful teases and shared giggles, replaced by a solemnity that seemed far too heavy for her young shoulders.

Through the eyes of a ten-year-old, she witnessed the unsettling effect of Misinformation, its ripples disturbing the tranquillity of her home. Despite her tender age, she was not unaffected. She found herself yearning for the return of the jovial spirit that usually graced their household, longing for the reassuring rhythm of their everyday life to resume.

Later that evening, the Kulkarni family sat together in their living room, the usual chatter replaced by an uneasy silence. The television blared in the background, News about the controversial article flashing across the screen.

A sudden buzz of Vijay's phone sliced through the thick silence in the room. It was a notification from Kapil, a blast from Vijay's past. A college friend who had chosen the path of Information Technology, he had a mind as sharp as a whip and an uncanny knack for sifting truth from the mirage of Misinformation. Kapil had sent a link, the digital equivalent of a lifeline tossed in the churning sea of chaos.

Vijay clicked on the link, filling his screen with an article. It was a fact-checking piece from a well-known and reliable news outlet, systematically debunking each claim made in the viral news article Vijay had shared earlier. The report was a meticulous dissection, each point carefully analyzed, cross-referenced and refuted with evidence. It was like watching a surgeon at work, each incision revealing more and more layers of deceit.

A heavy silence blanketed the room as Vijay took a deep breath, steadying himself, before reading aloud. Each word was a step towards the unsettling truth, each sentence a testament to the power and peril of Misinformation.

"Kapil's message," Vijay began, his voice steady, "is about the article I shared... It appears the information in it was false." He paused, letting the words sink in. He read out the fact-checked points one by one, the room absorbing the gravity of their situation.

On the other end of the line, Kapil offered his friend

reassurance. "Vijay, it's easy to get swayed. It happens to the best of us. It is important to learn from it and be more careful next time." His voice carried a mixture of sympathy and sternness, a gentle reminder of their responsibility as consumers and sharers of information.

The air in the room grew heavy. Vijay stared at the message from Kapil, his face pale. He glanced at his family, their eyes wide with shock, mirroring his feelings.

The room fell into an uneasy silence, the weight of realization settling over them like a thick blanket. Vijay, who had always been the pillar of strength, sat quietly, his brows furrowed as he grappled with the revelation. His eyes, usually filled with positive energy, bore a shadow of regret.

Finally, he stirred his voice barely a whisper, breaking through the tension in the room. "But how..." He swallowed, looking at each face around him, their expressions mirroring his confusion. "How could this have happened?"

He was holding his phone, the offending message still displayed on the screen. "I genuinely thought I was doing something good... something important," he admitted, the bitter taste of disillusionment seeping into his words.

A lump formed in Sangeeta's throat as she looked at Vijay. His words, heavy with regret, echoed the sentiments they all felt. They had been unknowing soldiers in an army of Misinformation, and the realization was a bitter pill to swallow.

Sangeeta reached out, taking his hand in hers. "We all make mistakes, Vijay," she said softly. "What matters is what we do next."

Vikrant, who had been quiet until now, spoke up. "Arjun also sent me a link debunking the article, Dad." He showed his phone to Vijay. "He said it's important to cross-check information before sharing it."
Vijay nodded, his mind racing. The situation was getting out of hand, the repercussions of his hasty decision-making themselves evident. He needed to make things right, but he needed to figure out where to start.

Just then, Sulochana tugged at Sangeeta's saree. "Mama," she asked, her voice filled with innocence and confusion, "Why is everyone upset about Papa's post?"

Sangeeta looked at her daughter, a thousand emotions running through her. How could she explain to a child the complex world of Misinformation? "Sometimes, sweetheart, people share News without checking if it's true. And that can cause problems. Like now with Papa's post."

Sulochana nodded, understanding as much as her young mind could.

The room was still shrouded in palpable silence, filled with a cocktail of regret and resolution. The quiet was abruptly shattered by the sharp buzz of Vijay's phone skidding across the polished wood of the coffee table. The screen lit up, displaying the name 'Sameer Gupta', a well-known reporter at one of the nation's most reputable news outlets and a friend of Vijay's for more years than he could count.

Vijay picked up the call, pressing the phone to his ear. His eyes widened slightly as he listened to Sameer's voice on the other end; a voice that usually held an easygoing charm was now laced with uncharacteristic seriousness.

"Vijay," Sameer said, his words punctuated by the occasional background noise of a bustling newsroom. "The story you shared... it's taken on a life of its own and picked up by other media houses."
A chill ran down Vijay's spine. He knew the power and reach of the media, and the thought of his shared post causing such a ripple was daunting.

"And it's going viral, Vijay," Sameer continued, the weight of his words hanging in the air. "And I don't mean that in the 'trending on social media way, and it's causing quite a stir and not looking good."

As Vijay ended the call, he set the phone back on the table, the screen's light casting long shadows on his face. The room was silent once again, but it wasn't just filled with regret this time. It was also filled with resolve. This was a lesson learned the hard way, but it was a lesson nonetheless.

The room spun around Vijay. His action, which seemed so trivial in the morning, had spiralled into something he had not anticipated. The post was not just affecting his close circle anymore; it was reaching a wider audience, creating ripples he never intended.

As he disconnected the call, he looked at his family, their faces a mirror of his own apprehension. "We're in the eye of a storm," he said, his voice heavy with regret. "And it's time we face it together."

And with that declaration, the Kulkarni family found themselves on a path they never expected to tread. Unbeknownst to them, this journey would change their lives forever, challenging their beliefs, relations, and understanding of the digital world they thought they knew so well.

This was their first step into the misinformation maze, a labyrinth they would have to navigate together. The dawn of the new day was about to bring challenges they never thought they would face in a world where truth and deception were two sides of the same coin.

CHAPTER TWO

The Viral Storm

The silence in the Kulkarni home was deafening, punctuated only by the occasional hum of the air conditioner and the ticking of the wall clock. The usual chatter, laughter, and warmth were replaced with a tense quietness. Each family member was wrapped in their own cocoon of thoughts, the morning events looming significant in their mind.

Vijay sat in his study, staring blankly at his computer screen. His thoughts wandered back to the morning's events – his excitement about sharing the News, the pride in his voice, the shock on his family's faces, and finally, Sameer's call. The memory of it sent a chill down his spine. His hands trembled slightly as he logged into his social media account. Notifications popped up by the dozens, each a grim reminder of the viral storm he had inadvertently created.

Across the hallway, Sangeeta sat on the edge of the bed in the master bedroom, worry etched on her face. Her mind was a whirlpool of concerns - about Vijay, the kids, their reputation, and the backlash from their extended family and friends. She remembered the pride in Vijay's voice that morning, the assurance with which he shared the News. It starkly contrasted with the man who sat in the study now - confused, regretful, and scared. She wished she could reach and comfort him, but the words eluded her.

Vikrant was in his room, his game console forgotten as he scrolled through his social media feed. His friends discussed the viral post, speculated about its origin, and shared memes. He felt guilt each time his father's name came up. He had seen his father's face fall when he had shown him the debunking link. He remembered the disappointment in his father's eyes, and it weighed heavy on his heart.

Little Sulochana, sitting on her bed with her favourite cartoon, paused on her tablet and could sense the tension in the house. She didn't understand the details, but she knew her father was upset about something he had shared on his phone. She felt a pit in her stomach as she thought about her usually cheerful father looking sad.

As the evening wore on, the doorbell rang. Kapil stood outside, a look of concern on his face. He had been in constant touch with Vijay throughout the day, offering advice, sharing updates, and trying to mitigate the damage.

As he stepped into the silent house, he felt the tension in the air. He looked at Vijay and the others, their faces a mirror of worry and regret.

Clearing his throat, he began, "We need to discuss this. We need a plan to handle this viral storm."
The family gathered around him as Kapil sat down in the

living room. His presence broke the icy silence that had engulfed the house.

The morning sun filtered through the curtains, casting long shadows on the Kulkarni's living room floor. Kapil, Vijay's old college friend and now an IT professional, had made his way to their house amidst the brewing crisis. His calm demeanour and familiarity with a decades-old friendship brought comfort to the household teetering on the edge of anxiety.

"Let's take a step back," Kapil suggested, his tone as steady as the gaze he fixed on Vijay. He was seated on the plush sofa, his posture relaxed, his face radiating an assurance that was much needed in the room. "Vijay, would you walk us through how you found this piece of news?"

Vijay shifted uncomfortably in his chair. The room was quiet, save for the ticking of the antique wall clock and the distant hum of city life outside their windows. It was in stark contrast to the chaos that had been unleashed online just a few hours ago.

With a deep breath, Vijay began his recount. "It was early in the morning... I was scrolling through my social media feed, just a regular start to my day..." His voice was shaky, reflecting the turmoil within him. He took them through the progression of events, from stumbling upon the news post to the adrenaline rush of urgency it sparked in him.

"I was concerned...it felt important... so, I shared it," Vijay's voice trailed off, the weight of the consequences of his impulsive action hung heavy in the room.

Ever the patient listener, Kapil nodded, his face softening in understanding. "It's alright, Vijay. We've all been there, and we must recognize these moments to learn how to tackle misinformation in the future."
After Vijay's account, Kapil turned to Vikrant. "You were the one who found out that the News was false, and can you explain how you figured it out?"

Vikrant explained his usual process of verifying any news before sharing, a habit he had cultivated from his early days as an aspiring YouTube influencer. He described how he cross-checked the News against multiple reliable sources and then confirmed it was false through a fact-checking website. His voice was steady, but there was a hint of guilt as he glanced at his father.

Sangeeta, who had been silent till now, finally voiced her concerns.

"But how did it spread so fast?

And why didn't anyone else check the information before sharing it?"

Kapil exhaled slowly, ruffling his slightly greying hair with a thoughtful hand. His gaze was distant as if he was looking beyond the confines of the room at the sprawling network of social media that had brought them to this situation.

"It's a double-edged sword, Sangeeta," Kapil began, turning his attention back to Vijay's wife. His tone blended concern and academic fascination, reflecting his deep understanding of the subject. "Social media has the incredible power to connect us, to bring us closer to friends and family, even when they're halfway across the globe. It allows us to share moments, ideas, and, yes, information."

"But therein lies the danger," Kapil continued, his gaze intense, "The ease of sharing information has outpaced our capacity to critically evaluate it. With a single click, a piece of information, whether true or false, can reach hundreds, thousands, even millions."

The room was quiet, everyone absorbed in Kapil's words, the gravity of the situation sinking further.
"And then, there's trust," Kapil added, his voice softer now. "We inherently trust our friends, our family, and we believe they wouldn't knowingly mislead us. So, when we receive information from them, our instinct isn't to question or verify it, but to accept it as truth."

He paused, letting the silence punctuate his words. "And that," he concluded, "is how misinformation spreads, not just by exploiting our biases, but also our trust and relationships."

Kapil paused momentarily before delving into his subsequent explanation, ensuring he had everyone's attention. He then began elucidating a complex mechanism that governs our virtual interactions.

"You see," Kapil started, "there's a term in social psychology - 'echo chamber'. In this situation, certain ideas, beliefs or data points are amplified or reinforced by repetition inside a defined system."

He glanced around the room, noticing the intrigued yet slightly confused faces. "Imagine being in a real echo chamber," he continued. "What you speak bounces back at you, right? A similar thing happens in the digital world, especially on social media platforms."

Kapil picked up his phone, a visual prop to aid his explanation. "The algorithms that control what we see on our feeds are designed to show us what we will likely engage with. So, suppose you often click on posts about gardening. In that case, you'll start seeing more gardening posts, tips, tools, groups, everything related to gardening."

Sangeeta interjected, "So, you're saying it's like creating a personalized world for us?"

"Exactly," Kapil nodded. "Now, extend this to our beliefs and views. The algorithm takes note if you have a certain political leaning or a stance on a social issue. You start seeing more content that aligns with your views. Over time, this can create a virtual echo chamber, where most of what you see and interact with aligns with your pre-existing beliefs."

"And the flip side," Kapil concluded, "is that you're less exposed to differing views, to challenging thoughts. Your belief is constantly reinforced and seldom questioned. That's how these echo chambers can contribute to spreading misinformation and make it challenging to debunk false narratives."

Vijay, pale, interjected, "But what do we do now? How do

we fix this?"

Kapil paused before answering. "First, we need to share a retraction, an apology. And then, we need to educate ourselves and others about the importance of verifying information before sharing it."

As the family discussed their action plan, Sulochana slipped into her room, her mind filled with adult conversations and heavy words. She didn't understand everything, but she understood one thing – her family was in trouble and fighting it together.

The night grew darker, and the discussions continued. The viral storm had hit the Kulkarni family, but they would not be swept away. They were standing their ground, ready to navigate through the misinformation maze.

Vijay's eyes flickered with determination as he prepared to face the situation head-on. "I will take responsibility for my mistake and issue the retraction," he affirmed, his voice steady, "But Kapil, how do we educate ourselves and others about this? I thought I was doing good by sharing that News."

Sangeeta nodded in agreement, her eyes mirroring the same question. Kapil leaned back, his gaze thoughtful. "That's a great question, Vijay, Sangeeta. It's not just about not sharing unverified News, and it's about understanding why we fall for such News in the first place."

Kapil started explaining cognitive biases and how our minds can trick us into believing misinformation. He spoke about confirmation bias, where we only listen to information that confirms our preconceptions, and the Dunning-Kruger effect, where people mistakenly assess their cognitive ability as more significant than it is.

Kapil, noticing the puzzled expressions on the faces of the family, decided to explain these complex concepts in simpler terms.

"Let's start with cognitive biases," he said, leaning forward. "Imagine you're trying to judge the distance of a ball thrown towards you, and you might misjudge it and get hit. That's an error in perception. Similarly, cognitive biases are errors in our thinking that occur when we process and interpret information in the world around us. They're like little mental shortcuts or 'rules of thumb' we use, which can sometimes lead us astray."

Vijay, Sangeeta, and Vikrant nodded, beginning to grasp the concept.

"Now, let's talk about confirmation bias. Imagine you believe it always rains when you forget your umbrella at home. Each time it rains, and you've forgotten your umbrella, you remember it clearly because it confirms your belief. But you likely ignore all the times it didn't rain when you forgot your umbrella or when it rained, and you had your umbrella. That's confirmation bias – our tendency to pay more attention to information that confirms our existing beliefs and ignore information that challenges them."

The room was silent as Kapil's explanation sank in. It was a simple concept, yet it was decisive in shaping their online experiences.

"And then there's the Dunning-Kruger effect," Kapil continued. "Let's say a person reads a few articles about a complex topic like climate change and then starts believing they're an expert. They start arguing with actual climate scientists, convinced that they know better. That's essentially the Dunning-Kruger effect – when someone overestimates their knowledge or competence in a particular area."

Vikrant chuckled, "I see that all the time online. People with little knowledge argue with experts, confident they're right."

Kapil nodded, "Exactly. And these biases and effects don't just occur in others. We all experience them to some degree. The first step towards navigating the misinformation maze is recognizing our biases."

Kapil's words echoed in the room, and the family shared thoughtful looks. The world of social media was beginning to unravel, revealing its intricate and often deceptive workings. The path through the misinformation maze was daunting. Still, with every conversation, every revelation, they were learning to chart their course.

Kapil's explanation sparked a light in Vikrant. He leaned forward, his eyes lit with the recognition of experiences that mirrored what Kapil described.

"You know," Vikrant began, the words tumbling out of him, "I've seen this first hand in the online gaming community.

Once, there was this rumour about a new game update, and it spread like wildfire."

He looked around, making sure everyone was following him before he continued. "There was no official announcement from the game developers. But someone had posted about it in a forum, and it caught on. People were excited about it, speculating on the features and sharing it in their circles. It was as if the update was real and happening."

The room was silent, all eyes on Vikrant. "I was sceptical," he continued. "So, I posted a message asking for the source of this information, questioning its authenticity."

Vikrant let out a small laugh, but there was a bitter edge to it. "I was met with a barrage of negative comments. I was called a party pooper, a troll, an attention seeker. Some even suggested leaving the community if I couldn't share their excitement."

He paused, looking a bit deflated. "It was eye-opening, and I realized that people didn't like their bubbles being burst. They were happy in their echo chamber, excited about the update, even if it might not be real."

Vikrant glanced at Kapil, a grim smile on his face. "It was then I understood the power of echo chambers, how they can shield us from reality, and how challenging it can be to break through them. It's not just about misinformation; it's about the comfort we derive from staying unchallenged and unquestioned."

As Kapil and Vikrant exchanged their experiences, Sangeeta was lost in a whirlwind of thoughts. She sat quietly in her armchair, her fingers nervously twirling a lock of her hair - a habit she had when deep in thought. The room around her, bathed in the soft glow of the table lamp, felt almost surreal. She could hear the rhythmic tick-tock of the wall clock, the occasional hum of a passing car, and the faint rustle of leaves outside the window. Still, all these seemed distant, muffled by the rush of information swirling in her mind.

In her perspective, social media had always been a benign entity - a fun, interactive platform where she shared snippets of her life, exchanged pleasantries, and kept in touch with friends and family. She enjoyed the pleasant surprises it often presented - an old school friend sending a friend request, a heartwarming video of a dog playing with a baby, or a beautifully written poem that touched her heart. It was her window to the world, a world that was most kind, engaging, and comforting.

But now, as she listened to Kapil and Vikrant, she felt like a veil had been lifted, revealing a more complex, intricate, and somewhat darker landscape. The same platform she found harmless and inviting was used to spread misinformation, create divisions, and manipulate opinions. She was looking at a familiar painting but seeing new, disconcerting details that she had previously missed or ignored.

The realization was unnerving, and a pang of unease gnawed at her. She glanced at her phone on the coffee table, its screen dark and silent. It felt different, almost alien. She felt a sudden urgency to understand, learn, and adapt. For herself, her family, and the world her daughter Sulochana would inherit. She understood that The quest for truth was not just Vijay's journey but hers.

Even Sulochana, who had snuck back into the living room, her curiosity piqued, listened with wide-eyed attention. The conversations and heavy words all painted a picture of an online world much more considerable and scarier than her cartoon-filled universe.

The clock struck midnight, marking the end of a long, stressful day. As the family members retreated to their rooms, their minds were filled with thoughts. The viral storm had stirred up more than just trouble - it had sparked questions, revealed truths, and started conversations.

The Kulkarni family was still in the eye of the storm, but they were no longer helpless. Armed with new knowledge and a determination to set things right, they prepared themselves to face the new day. The viral storm was yet to pass, but they were ready to weather it together. The path through the misinformation maze was still unclear, but they had taken their first steps towards finding their way out.

CHAPTER THREE

The Quest for Truth

The morning sun streamed through the windows of the Kulkarni residence, casting long shadows on the floor. The house was tranquil, and each family member was lost in their thoughts. The previous day's events had plunged them into a whirlpool of introspection, and they were each grappling with their own realizations.

Vijay sat at the dining table, his breakfast untouched, his gaze lost in the steam rising from his tea. The sting of the previous day's revelations still echoed in his mind. He replayed Kapil's words about cognitive biases and realized he had been a victim. He had allowed his beliefs to cloud his judgement and his desire for validation to override the truth. The realization was bitter, but Vijay acknowledged it with a resigned nod.

Sangeeta, watching Vijay from the kitchen, felt a pang of sympathy. She knew her husband was a good man who had been caught unawares by the complexities of the digital world. She pondered over Kapil's words too. How often had she shared a recipe or a health tip without verifying its authenticity, assuming it was true because it came from a trusted friend? The thought made her uncomfortable.

In his room, Vikrant was scrolling through his social media feeds with a newfound perspective. He saw the biases Kapil had spoken about everywhere - in the shared news articles, comments, and heated discussions. It was like he had been given a pair of glasses that revealed the hidden layers of the online world.

Even little Sulochana was not immune to the change. She sat with her favourite cartoons playing on the TV, but her mind was elsewhere. She thought about the overheard discussions and wondered if her cartoons also had any of this "miss...info...nation".

Amid this quiet introspection, the ringing phone cut through the silence. It was Sameer, the reporter's friend from Delhi. His enthusiastic voice boomed through the phone, "Vijay, I heard about what happened. But don't worry, we'll turn this around."

And thus began the Kulkarni family's quest for truth. Each day, guided by Kapil and Sameer, they delved deeper into the workings of social media, the mechanisms of Misinformation, and the techniques to fact-check and verify News. They began to question, to probe, to think critically. They learned to step out of their comfort zones, challenge their biases, and appreciate the importance of diverse perspectives. It was a transformation journey, unlearning and relearning, and coming together as a family.

The quest for truth took work. There were moments of frustration, of disbelief, of heated debates. But there were also moments of enlightenment, understanding, and collective triumphs. Each hurdle they overcame, each bias they identified, and each piece of Misinformation they debunked brought them one step closer to navigating the misinformation maze.

As the sun set on yet another day of their quest, the Kulkarni family sat together in the living room, a sense of camaraderie filling the air. They were not just a family anymore. They were a team united by their quest for truth, their resolve to learn, and their determination to make a difference. And they knew their journey had only just begun.

There was a palpable sense of anticipation as they gathered in the living room that evening. Vijay broke the silence, "We have been learning so much. But how do we take this forward? What can we do to counter Misinformation?"

Sangeeta nodded in agreement, "I have been thinking about the same. We've been passive consumers, but it's time we become more active."

Vikrant chimed in, "Maybe we can start with our own networks. Make our friends and family aware of these biases, of how to fact-check information before sharing."

Sulochana, wide-eyed, asked, "Does that mean we need to become detectives?"

They all laughed at her innocent question, but Kapil, who was on a video call with them, smiled and said, "In a way, yes, Sulochana. We all need to become 'information detectives."

With a newfound sense of responsibility, the Kulkarni family embarked on the next chapter of their journey - the mission of enlightenment and outreach. Their dinner table conversations evolved from passive discussions to strategizing sessions, with each member eagerly chipping in with their ideas and plans.

Vijay, whose business network spanned across different industries and regions, took it upon himself to introduce this crucial subject to his professional circle. He began by sending out a carefully worded email to his contacts, explaining his recent experiences and the insights he gained about Misinformation. He urged them to be vigilant and to adopt a habit of questioning and verifying any information before passing it on. His message was well-received, and many of his contacts appreciated his initiative, some even promising to carry it to their own networks.

Meanwhile, Sangeeta, who significantly influenced her teacher's group, decided to use her platform effectively. She initiated conversations about the prevalence and dangers of Misinformation in their group meetings and shared resources to verify the information. She even proposed including media literacy in their school curriculum, a suggestion met with enthusiastic approval.

Vikrant, the gaming enthusiast with a substantial online presence, took a different approach. He realized that the gaming community, with its vast and diverse user base, was a fertile ground for Misinformation. He started a campaign on his gaming forum, using engaging infographics and video snippets to illustrate the importance of fact-checking. He shared tips on how to identify credible sources and debunk false claims. His posts were shared widely within the community, sparking conversations about responsible information sharing.

As each day passed, the family felt fulfilled seeing their efforts taking shape. They understood that the battle against Misinformation was not a sprint but a marathon. Yet, they were prepared and determined to keep going.

As the Kulkarni family ventured into these conversations, they were met with a spectrum of reactions. Some resisted their efforts, clinging tightly to their beliefs and dismissing the family's attempts to dispel Misinformation as unnecessary meddling. They endured scornful remarks and even open hostility, with some accusing them of trying to suppress certain narratives.

Vijay had a particularly rough exchange with an old business associate who refused to acknowledge the existence of Misinformation, branding it as a "myth". Sangeeta was met with scoffs from a few members of her teacher's group, who found her emphasis on media literacy to be an overreaction. Vikrant faced online trolls who targeted him for disrupting their echo chamber with his campaign.

However, amid the pushback, they also encountered individuals who were receptive to their message. They found allies who echoed their concerns about Misinformation and supporters who appreciated their efforts. Vijay's email sparked thoughtful discussions among his business circle. A couple of teachers in Sangeeta's group came forward to help her draft a proposal for media literacy in the school curriculum. Vikrant's posts on responsible information sharing were met with positive responses, and many gamers expressed their gratitude for his efforts.

While discussing their experiences one day, Sameer suggested, "Why not document your journey? Share your experiences, your learnings, your triumphs, and your setbacks. It could inspire others to embark on their own quests for truth."

The idea resonated with the family, and they started a blog - "The Misinformation Maze: A Family's Quest for Truth". They took turns writing posts, sharing anecdotes, debunking common myths, and explaining concepts simply. The blog soon gained traction and started receiving appreciation from readers who found it helpful and inspiring.

The Kulkarni family underwent a profound transformation as their quest for truth advanced. No longer were they merely passive recipients of information in the digital world; they had evolved into vigilant guardians, actively questioning and examining the News and stories they encountered. They had traversed from being susceptible targets of Misinformation to becoming resilient bastions of truth.

Vijay found himself scrutinizing every piece of News he came across, cross-referencing it with other sources, and verifying its authenticity before accepting or sharing it. Sangeeta was now a fervent advocate of media literacy, incorporating it into her teaching and spreading awareness among her colleagues. Vikrant, ever active in his online gaming community, used his digital influence to promote responsible information sharing and discourage the spread of unverified rumours.

What they initially perceived as a maze of Misinformation was now seen as a labyrinth with patterns and signs. They learned to decipher these signs with each stride, navigate the convoluted paths, and confront the monstrous Minotaur of Misinformation. They had equipped themselves with the sword of critical thinking and the shield of fact-checking, ready to face the challenges ahead.

Their transformation was both empowering and humbling. They recognized the power they wielded as information sharers and the responsibility that came with it. The road ahead was long and winding, and they knew their journey had only begun. It was as though they stood at the mouth of the labyrinth, peering into its depths, ready to delve deeper into the fight against Misinformation. With renewed resolve, the Kulkarni family marched forward, their hearts filled with courage and their minds armed with knowledge.

A few weeks had passed since they had launched their blog, and the response was overwhelming. They received comments from people worldwide, thanking them for their insight and sharing their experiences. This was their confirmation that they were on the right path.

One evening, during their regular gathering in the living room, Vijay brought up a comment he had read on the blog. "There was a comment from a reader who mentioned how they fell victim to a health scam online, and it took them a long time to realize they were duped. They expressed gratitude for our efforts to educate people about Misinformation."

Sangeeta looked thoughtful. "That's disturbing but not surprising. Health misinformation is rampant, and even I had shared a few without thinking about their authenticity."

Sangeeta's thoughtful expression deepened as she pondered over the reader's comment. She remembered her own experiences with health misinformation, which now felt like lessons in gullibility.

"I remember," she began, her voice soft, "when I came across this post about a 'miracle' cure for arthritis. It was a simple herbal concoction, and the post claimed it was a traditional remedy passed down generations. The post was well-written, with many positive comments, and even had a few before-and-after pictures. It seemed so authentic that I didn't think twice before sharing it with my friends suffering from arthritis."
Her voice trailed off as she recalled the embarrassment she felt when a friend, who was a doctor, politely informed her that the 'miracle cure' was, in fact, a well-known internet hoax.

"Looking back, I realize I should have been more sceptical," she admitted. "The post had no references to any studies or credible sources and was all anecdotal evidence. But the promise of an easy, natural remedy was so tempting, it clouded my judgment."

Sangeeta sighed, "Health misinformation is dangerous because it preys on people's fears and hopes. It's easy to get carried away when you're desperate for a cure or an easy fix. And the worst part is, it's not just on social media, and I've seen it being shared on family and friends groups on WhatsApp, too."

"But that's in the past," she said, a new determination in her voice. "Now, we know better. We know how to verify information, look for credible sources, and, most importantly, understand the responsibility of sharing information. We have a long way to go, but we're making progress."

Her words hung in the air, a testament to their shared journey. The Kulkarni family had indeed come a long way. From being passive information consumers to becoming active seekers of truth, their journey was a testament to the power of knowledge and the will to learn.

Vikrant silently followed the conversation, his brows furrowed in deep thought. He was typically the most vocal in the family but reticent tonight. The discussion had struck a chord with him. His silence broke, and with a rare seriousness for the usually spirited teenager, he said, "You know, it's not just health-related information that gets twisted. Even in gaming communities, Misinformation is rampant."

The family looked at him in surprise. Gaming and Misinformation were not two words they expected to hear in the same sentence. Seeing their puzzled expressions,

Vikrant elaborated.

"About a year ago, there was this rumour about a major update for one of my favourite games. It was supposed to introduce a new character with some incredible abilities. The rumour spread like wildfire in the gaming community. YouTube was flooded with videos discussing strategies for the new character. The forums were filled with excited discussions, and everyone eagerly awaited the update. I was swept up in the excitement, too," he confessed.

"But then the update day came, and there was no new character. It was all a hoax, a false rumour started by someone for reasons unknown. To stir up the gaming community or for some twisted fun. It was a letdown for all of us who had been waiting. But more than that, it was a stark realization of how easy it was to spread Misinformation."

Vikrant's voice echoed in the room, each word hanging heavy with disappointment and newfound wisdom. "Now I know better," he said, a firm resolve in his voice. "I double-check any news I hear, especially if it sounds too good. And I try to inform others when they fall for such rumours."

The room was silent as they absorbed Vikrant's words. It was a stark reminder that Misinformation was not limited to severe issues like health or politics. It was everywhere, touching all aspects of life, even areas that seemed as innocuous as a video game. The pervasiveness of Misinformation was alarming, but as Vikrant's experience showed, it was something they could learn to navigate with awareness and discernment.

Kapil had been following the family's discussion closely over the video call, his face illuminated by the soft glow of the computer screen. He had been silently nodding along, his eyes reflecting his deep understanding of the problem. When Vikrant finished his tale, Kapil leaned closer to the camera, his eyes serious.

"Misinformation doesn't discriminate," he began, his voice steady over the call. "It's not just about health, politics, or gaming, and it's everywhere. It affects everyone, regardless of their interests or demographics."
His voice was strong, the words spoken with the conviction of someone who had seen the effects of Misinformation first-hand in his IT career. "In my line of work, I've seen Misinformation cause businesses to make wrong decisions, students choose incorrect paths, and people develop unjustified fears. It preys on people's biases, hopes, and fears."

He paused, allowing the weight of his words to sink in before continuing, "But the more we learn and share, the better equipped we become to handle it."

His message was one of empowerment. "Every time we question a piece of information, every time we verify before sharing, every time we educate others about the importance of these actions, we're building our defence against misinformation."

He held up his hand, fingers outstretched, "Think of it like your hand. Each finger is a strategy - questioning, verifying, educating, staying informed, and adapting. Alone, they're helpful. But when you clench them together into a fist, they become a powerful force."

As Kapil's words filled the room, they brought with them a sense of determination.

Sameer, who was also on the call, added, "That's true. As journalists, we deal with this daily. The important thing is to stay curious, ask questions, and verify the source. And most importantly, not to feel embarrassed or ashamed if we ever fall for Misinformation. It happens to the best of us and is a learning process."
The family found comfort and strength in these words. They realized the importance of their mission - not just for themselves but for everyone touched by Misinformation. They made a pact to continue their quest for truth and to make a difference, one blog post at a time.

And so, the quest continued. The Kulkarni family, united by their pursuit of truth, became a beacon of hope in their community. They showed that anyone could become an information detective' with the proper knowledge and determination. As they ventured further into the depths of the misinformation maze, they held onto the belief that they were making a difference, however small it may be. Their quest for truth was just getting started, and they were ready for whatever lay ahead.

CHAPTER FOUR

The Echo Chamber Effect

The morning sun streamed through the Kulkarni's living room window, casting long shadows on the floor. The usually bustling household was tranquil, and Sangeeta was engrossed in an article on her tablet. Vikrant was glued to his gaming console, and Vijay was lost in the morning newspaper. The silence was broken by a ping from Sangeeta's tablet.

A sudden, sharp intake of breath shattered the silence in the room. "Oh, heavens!" Sangeeta's voice, tinged with shock and dread, echoed ominously around the otherwise quiet space.

The rustling of papers ceased abruptly, and Vijay and Vikrant, both startled by the sudden distress in her voice, swivelled their heads towards her. Their eyes, wide with concern, met the chilling sight of Sangeeta's face drained of its usual colour, her eyes reflecting a mixture of fear and confusion.

She clutched her phone tightly, its screen glowing

ominously in the dim evening light. "This article," she began, her voice shaky, "it says that our local hospital is running out of vaccines." Her voice trailed off, and she gulped, the significance of those words hanging heavily in the room.

Sangeeta's statement hit them like a thunderbolt. The local hospital - the one they had put their faith in, the one where they had scheduled their vaccinations next week - was running out of vaccines? Their hearts sank.

Vijay and Vikrant exchanged a startled glance, the same troubling thought registering in their minds. The atmosphere in the room became thick with worry, their previous conversations about Misinformation now taking on a stark, personal relevance. The family's anxiety was palpable, the unsettling news article casting a dark shadow over their evening.

Vijay, always the voice of reason, calmly suggested, "Maybe we should verify this information before panicking. Kapil was telling us about this, remember?"

Sangeeta nodded, remembering their conversation the previous night. She quickly sent the article to Kapil, asking for his help verifying the information.

Kapil called back in a few minutes, his face serious. "This is a perfect example of an echo chamber effect," he said. Seeing the puzzled look on their faces, he explained, "An echo chamber is a situation where certain ideas, beliefs or data points are amplified or reinforced by communication and repetition inside a defined system or group of people.

It's like being in a bubble where you only hear views or beliefs like yours. This can often lead to Misinformation or a skewed perspective."

As they listened, Kapil continued. "In this case, the article is based on a single source and is circulated among a specific group, causing unnecessary panic. The hospital has issued a statement clarifying that they have sufficient vaccines. The echo chamber makes a small issue seem like a major crisis."

He paused, letting his words sink in. "We must be cautious about echo chambers, especially on social media. They can distort our understanding of reality and can lead to polarized views. Always cross-verify information, especially if it's causing fear or panic."

The Kulkarnis listened intently. Their journey was proving to be a learning experience, not just about the dangers of Misinformation but also about their own biases and behaviour. The echo chamber effect was another hurdle to overcome, another lesson to learn in their quest for truth.

The silence that followed Kapil's explanation was palpable. Sangeeta looked at her tablet screen, her face a mix of relief and bewilderment. She had unknowingly become part of an echo chamber, and the realization was unnerving.

Vikrant broke the silence, "So, that's how these rumours spread, huh?" He looked at his console, thinking about his gaming community and the rumours that often circulated there. "I guess we gamers are also trapped in our echo chambers."

Kapil, appearing like a sage on the screen, nodded sagely. His words flowed with the calmness of a quiet river, yet they carried the weight of a crashing wave. "Vikrant, you're spot on," he began, his gaze firm and steady. "Echo chambers aren't limited to the domains of news or politics. They can, and do, permeate any community, including the seemingly innocuous gaming world."

He paused momentarily, letting his words sink in, his fingers gently tapping on the table to an inaudible rhythm. "Think about it," he continued, "In your gaming groups, you're likely surrounded by people who share your enthusiasm for the same games, strategies, and gaming platforms. This isn't a problem, but it could limit your exposure to different perspectives and ideas."

As Kapil spoke, Vikrant found himself nodding along, his previous encounters with gaming rumours and biases now making perfect sense in this new light. The concept of echo chambers in gaming communities, which had seemed abstract and distant, suddenly felt relevant and accurate.

"But how do we do that?" Sulochana asked, her young mind grappling with the weight of the topic. "How do we step out of our echo chamber?"

Kapil's face lit up at Sulochana's curiosity, a sign of the proactive approach they aimed to inculcate. "Well, Sulochana," he began, his voice resonating with an encouraging warmth, "you can commence by diversifying your social media circle. Follow people with a wide range of perspectives, not just those whose views align with yours or those who share your interests."

He gestured with his hands as if painting a broad landscape before her. "Immerse yourself in a variety of reading materials from diverse sources. Don't limit yourself to one viewpoint; explore multiple angles on the same topic. You'll be surprised at how different yet interconnected these perspectives can be."

Kapil's gaze met Sulochana's, his earnestness mirrored in her attentive eyes. "Critical thinking is key, Sulochana. Don't just consume information; question it. Engage in healthy debates, challenge ideas and let your ideas be challenged. This exchange of thoughts, this intellectual spar, is how we grow and learn."

Finally, he leaned in slightly as if sharing a secret. "And perhaps the most crucial step of all - always verify the information before you share it. It's tempting to hit that share button, especially when the information seems important or urgent. But remember, a few minutes spent on verification can prevent the spread of false information. The truth is worth that wait, wouldn't you agree?"

His words hung in the air, a beacon of guidance for the young mind, a roadmap for her journey through the labyrinth of information that lay ahead.

As Kapil's advice echoed in the room, each Kulkarni family member reflected on their social media habits. They realized it wasn't just about navigating Misinformation but also about breaking free from their echo chambers and opening their minds to different perspectives. And this was just the beginning. As they continued their quest for truth, they knew they would stumble upon more such revelations, each teaching them something new about the world and, more importantly, themselves. And with each revelation, they were one step closer to finding their way through the maze of Misinformation.

Vijay, who had been listening to the conversation with a furrowed brow, finally chimed in, "This echo chamber... it's like being in a room full of mirrors, reflecting only what you want to see."

"An apt analogy," Kapil responded, his face lighting up on the screen. "And just like a room full of mirrors, it can distort your perception. But the good thing is, once you know its existence, you can work towards breaking free."

"But isn't it normal to want to connect with like-minded people? People who share our interests?" Sangeeta asked, looking pensive.

Kapil paused to gather his thoughts before continuing, "Think of it like this, Sangeeta. Imagine you're in a garden full of roses. The roses are beautiful, and you love them because they align with your preference for beauty. But if you stay in this garden of roses, you're missing out on the other types of flowers that are just as beautiful, if not more so. You don't get to experience the delight of a blooming tulip, or the charm of a sunflower, or the elegance of an orchid."

Kapil's words hung as he let the metaphor sink in.

"In the same way," he continued, "when we surround ourselves only with people who share our views and interests, we deprive ourselves of the richness of diverse perspectives. We get so used to hearing and seeing what we want that we believe that's the only truth. We stop questioning, stop challenging our own beliefs, and that's where the problem arises."

Sangeeta's head moved up and down in a slow nod, her mind processing the depth of Kapil's words. A mental picture of her online world started forming before her eyes. She was integral to the close-knit groups - her cooking circle, the neighbourhood women's association, and the book club. The pages she followed, each one a mirror reflecting her hobbies and passions - wellness forums, gardening enthusiasts, DIY crafts. The people she interacted with online had profiles aligned with her ideologies and sensibilities.

In this virtual space, she had built a comforting echo chamber, a garden of roses where everything was familiar and pleasant. Each post she interacted with, each story she shared, was like a rose that matched the hues of her garden, reinforcing her existing beliefs and preferences.

But now, Kapil's words echoed in her mind, nudging her to step beyond her rose-tinted world. To seek out the daisies and the tulips, to appreciate the diversity of the floral world beyond her own. Had she ever considered stepping out of this comfortable enclosure? Had she ever consciously sought different perspectives or invited a viewpoint that didn't align with hers?

Her own thoughts surprised her. She realized she had been cocooned within her self-created echo chamber, oblivious to the multitude of voices and narratives outside her virtual garden. This realization was unsettling, yet it opened her eyes to the vast expanse of the digital world, teeming with diverse perspectives and ideas waiting to be explored.

"And when we're only hearing and seeing what we want," Kapil said, "we become easy targets for Misinformation. Because if someone feeds us a lie that aligns with our existing beliefs, we're more likely to believe it without questioning. That's how bias works, and that's how Misinformation spreads."

The weight of Kapil's words settled on them. The echo chamber was not just a concept anymore; it was a reality they had been living, a truth they had to confront.

Vikrant, absorbed in the conversation, looked up from his console. "So, we need to balance our sources of information. Mix up our social media feed, maybe follow some fact-checking sites?"

Kapil leaned forward; his expression was solemn as he delved deeper into the concept. "You see, we live in a world where information is just a click away. But this accessibility is a double-edged sword. While it allows us to learn and grow, it can also inundate us with Misinformation if we're not careful."

His gaze shifted between the Kulkarni family members on the screen, ensuring they followed along. "Take, for instance, a simple message forwarded on a social media

group, which may seem harmless and helpful.
But have you ever stopped to wonder where that information came from?

Who is the original source?

Is it credible?"

Vikrant's brows knitted together, the echo of past encounters with Misinformation in his gaming universe reverberating in his mind. He recalled rumours about new game releases, manipulated accounts of player controversies, and misrepresented statistics - a whirlwind of unverified information that he, too, had unknowingly been a part of spreading within his gaming community. The weight of his realization was palpable.

In stark contrast, Sulochana, at the tender age of ten, found herself contemplating the countless messages that arrived in her social media inbox daily. Funny memes, heartwarming animal videos, shocking news headlines, and even miraculous health tips - her digital universe was vibrant. Still, now, it could be misleading. Even as a child, she understood that not everything she saw or read could be taken at face value.

Across the room, Sangeeta and Vijay locked eyes, their expressions reflecting a shared understanding. The repercussions of Misinformation had left an indelible mark on their lives and their community. Kapil's words resonated deeply, creating ripples of thought and nudging them towards a more conscious and responsible approach to consuming and sharing information.

At that moment, a shared silence enveloped the Kulkarni family. Despite their age and experience, each member found themselves grappling with a new reality. Their roles in the spread of Misinformation, their newfound insights, and their collective resolve to be part of the solution cast a profound resonance in the room. The conversation with Kapil had been more than just enlightening; it was a compass guiding them towards responsible digital citizenship.

"You see," Kapil continued, "it's not enough to consume information. In this digital information age, we must also become responsible information disseminators. And for that, critical thinking is crucial."

He held up a finger for emphasis. "Before sharing any information, ask yourself -

Is this information verified?

Does it come from a credible source?

Is it backed by evidence?

If you're unsure, it's better to refrain from sharing it."

He paused, letting his words sink in. "Remember, whenever you share unverified information, you become a part of the misinformation chain. But every time you question, verify, and share information, you become a part of the solution."

The message was clear and potent. It was about navigating the information jungle and becoming responsible citizens in the digital world.

The conversation continued, each family member taking turns sharing their thoughts, concerns, and plans to step out of their echo chambers. The Kulkarnis, once again, found themselves at the threshold of a new understanding, ready to face the challenge head-on. As the sun set outside, casting an orange glow in their living room, they knew their quest for truth had become more exciting and authentic. Their journey through the maze of Misinformation was beginning to unravel.

CHAPTER FIVE

The Expert's Advice

The screen flickered, the pixels rearranging themselves into the face of Mr Swaminathan, their guide for the information jungle. His eyes were kind, framed by laugh lines that hinted at a life spent in earnest pursuits. Even through the digital medium, he exuded an aura of wisdom.

"Namaste, Kulkarni family," he greeted, his voice holding the warmth of a seasoned teacher. "I hear you've been on quite a journey."

Vijay cleared his throat, a bit nervous. "Yes, Mr. Swaminathan. We realized we've been living in an echo chamber, unaware of the rampant Misinformation."

Sangeeta joined in, "We've started questioning, verifying the information we come across. But it's sometimes overwhelming, and we are unsure if we're doing it right."

Vikrant and Sulochana nodded, their faces mirroring their parents' concern. Sitting quietly in the corner of the screen, Kapil watched the exchange with interest.

Mr Swaminathan's features softened as a gentle smile

played on his lips, his eyes twinkling like distant stars with an underlying hint of pride. "I appreciate your candidness," he began, his voice carrying an undertone of reassurance that seemed to wrap around the room, easing the tension and encouraging a sense of hope.

He leaned back in his chair, his hands folded in his lap, his gaze steady on the Kulkarni family. "Remember, in any journey towards change, the first and perhaps the most daunting step is acknowledging the existence of a problem. It's like standing at the edge of a vast, intimidating forest, unsure of the path ahead."

His smile widened slightly as he continued, "But the fact that you've recognized there's a problem means you've already taken that first crucial step. You've acknowledged the forest and are ready to venture into it."

He paused, letting his words sink in, and a comforting silence enveloped the room. "Now," he said, his tone firm yet inviting, "we won't just stand at the edge. We will walk together, navigating this forest of Misinformation. We'll tread the path of discernment, understanding, and truth."

His powerful and encouraging words filled the room with a newfound determination. The Kulkarni family, once victims of Misinformation, now found themselves on the cusp of becoming warriors of truth, and they knew they were not alone in their journey.

The Kulkarni leaned in, eager for the wisdom about to be shared.

Mr Swaminathan's voice echoed through the speakers, commanding attention. He leaned forward, his hands clasped together, and started explaining the complexities of Misinformation.

"Let's start with the primary characteristic of misinformation," Mr Swaminathan began, his voice a steady, calming presence in the room. "It has an uncanny ability to blend in, to present itself as the truth."
He shifted in his seat, locking eyes with the Kulkarni family, ensuring he had their undivided attention. "Imagine it like a chameleon. It adapts its colours to its surroundings, making it difficult to distinguish from its environment. Similarly, Misinformation is dressed in the garb of truth, woven with threads of reality that make it seem logical and credible. Its most dangerous trait is the ability to hide in plain sight."

To illustrate his point, he started giving examples. "Take, for instance, a misquoted statement. In a speech, a renowned scientist mentions that 'more research is needed to understand the full effects of a particular drug.' Now, if someone takes only a part of this statement, say, 'the full effects of the drug are not understood,' it completely changes the meaning and creates unnecessary panic. The original context is lost, and the statement, although partly true, becomes misleading."

He continued, "Or consider a photograph - an image of a protest, for instance. With today's advanced software, it's easy to manipulate the image to look like there's violence when there is none. Although based on a real event, the image has been distorted to spread a false narrative."

Lastly, he delved into the concept of news manipulation. "A factual event can be framed in a way that completely shifts its context. For example, a peaceful demonstration might be reported as a violent riot, simply by focusing on a minor scuffle and ignoring the broader peaceful gathering."

Mr Swaminathan's examples hung in the air, highlighting the intricate web of Misinformation, showing how easy it was for the truth to be distorted and how vigilant one must be to navigate the maze of information.
He paused, giving them a moment to absorb the information. He then picked up the thread of his explanation once again, this time focusing on the psychological aspect of Misinformation.

"Confirmation bias," he started, "is a mental shortcut that our brains use to make sense of the world. It's our tendency to favour information that aligns with our existing beliefs or prejudices. We're more likely to accept, share, and remember information that fits our worldview and dismiss anything that contradicts it."
He leaned forward, his eyes gleaming with a profound intensity. "Misinformation exploits this flaw in our thinking process. It doesn't aim to provide a balanced view. Instead, it presents a skewed narrative that echoes our pre-existing notions, making it seem more believable to us."

To illustrate his point, he harked back to the examples shared earlier. "Consider the misquoted statement scenario. Suppose you already harbour scepticism towards the drug in question. In that case, you are more likely to believe and share the misquoted statement that 'the full effects of the drug are not understood,' even though it's out of context."

"Or take the manipulated image of a peaceful protest turned violent. Suppose you already have a bias against the protestors. In that case, you are more likely to accept the manipulated image as truth and even share it, feeding the cycle of Misinformation."

"And finally, the news manipulation. Suppose you already hold a negative view of the group holding the demonstration. In that case, you are more likely to believe the skewed report of a peaceful demonstration as a violent riot."

He let the silence linger, giving the Kulkarni family time to understand the role their own biases could play in falling prey to Misinformation. The examples, grounded in everyday life, highlighted how easily one could be swept up in Misinformation if one did not stay vigilant and question their biases.

The Kulkarni family listened attentively as Mr Swaminathan said, "Then there's apophenia, the human tendency to perceive connections and meaningful patterns between unrelated things. Misinformation exploits this by linking unrelated events or facts to create a convincing narrative."

Mr Swaminathan, seeing their rapt attention, decided to expand further on the concept of apophenia. "Let's imagine this," he began, his voice steady and clear. "You see a news piece about a celebrity who fell ill shortly after eating at a particular restaurant. Later that day, you come across a social media post claiming that the same restaurant uses poor-quality ingredients. You immediately connect the two incidents in your mind and believe the restaurant to be the cause of the celebrity's illness."

He paused, allowing the family to digest the example. "This is a classic case of apophenia. You've connected two unrelated pieces of information to form a meaningful pattern - in this case, a narrative that blames the restaurant for the celebrity's illness. But correlation doesn't necessarily mean causation. The celebrity could have fallen ill due to numerous other reasons unrelated to the restaurant."

He continued, "Misinformation often exploits this tendency. It presents unrelated facts or events in a way that encourages you to form a connection between them. This connection, although compelling, is often misleading."

Vikrant nodded thoughtfully, the teenager's face showing a newfound understanding. Sangeeta and Vijay, too, were absorbing the implications of this insight, their expressions reflective. They could now see how easy it was to be led astray by Misinformation and how important it was to question and verify before accepting any narrative at face value.

Mr Swaminathan's voice took on a tone of practicality as he began outlining the techniques to counter Misinformation.

"Fact-checking," he reiterated, "is your first line of defence. It's the process of questioning the accuracy of a piece of information, be it a statement, an image, or a news report."

He leaned back in his chair, a thoughtful expression on his face. "Let's take an example. You come across a news article claiming a certain celebrity has made a controversial statement. Don't accept it at face value because it's written in a news article. Look for other sources reporting on the same incident. Is the statement reported consistently across different outlets? Or are there variations?"

His fingers danced in the air as he counted off the points. "Look for primary sources if possible. In this case, if there's a video of the celebrity making the statement, that would be a primary source. But remember to watch the whole video, not just the part quoted in the article. Context is important."

"Secondly, there are various fact-checking websites available that can help you validate a piece of information," he continued, reaching for his tablet. "Websites like Snopes, FactCheck.org, or AFP Fact Check specialize in debunking false claims, rumours, and fake News. They use rigorous methods to cross-check information, giving you a reliable verdict on its authenticity."

His fingers swiped across the screen, pulling up one of the mentioned websites. "Let me show you an example. Here's a claim that was circulating recently about a meteorite predicted to hit Earth. Sounds scary, right? But if we check it on this fact-checking site, we can see they've debunked it. The claim was based on a misinterpretation of a NASA announcement. In reality, the meteorite will pass safely by Earth."

With these examples and tools, Mr Swaminathan illustrated the importance of fact-checking and verification. He handed the family a toolkit to navigate the treacherous waters of Misinformation, urging them to question, verify, and think critically before accepting any information as truth.

Mr Swaminathan's expression turned earnest as he reached his next point, recognizing credible sources.
"Identifying credible sources of information is just as important as fact-checking," he stressed. "Credible sources will usually come from reputable organizations or individuals with proven expertise in the field."

He clasped his hands together and leaned forward, his gaze engaging each of them in turn. "For instance, let's say you come across an article claiming a new breakthrough in cancer research. Now, who is the author of this article? Is it a renowned oncologist or a journalist specializing in health and science reporting? Or is it written by someone without evident expertise in the field?"

His eyes sparkled with a hint of challenge. "And where is the article published? Is it on a reputable news website or a scientific journal? Or is it on a blog that anyone could create and publish?"

He paused, letting the questions hang in the air before continuing. "Reputable sources, like The New York Times, BBC, or scientific journals such as Nature or The Lancet, have rigorous editorial standards and fact-checking processes. The authors of their articles are usually experts in their fields or journalists with experience in the topic they are covering."

"The same goes for the author," he added. "A renowned oncologist or a health journalist will have the necessary knowledge and expertise to write accurately about a new breakthrough in cancer research. They will likely cite their sources, allowing you to check the original research yourself."

He leaned back, surveying the family. "When you evaluate the source and the author, you can gauge the reliability of the information. Remember, anyone can publish anything on the internet. It's up to us to discern the credible from the non-credible."

Mr Swaminathan's explanation painted a clear picture. In the world of information, not all sources are created equal. Some are credible, built on expertise, rigorous processes, and a commitment to truth, and others are not. Recognizing this distinction was another step in navigating the misinformation maze.

Finally, he delved into the concept of biased reporting. "Biased reporting presents facts in a way that leans towards a particular viewpoint, often leaving out opposing perspectives. It's crucial to understand this and to seek out information from diverse sources to get a balanced view."

Mr Swaminathan elaborated on biased reporting, his voice steady and clear. "Let's consider a simple example to understand this. Imagine there's a news story about a protest. One news outlet might focus on the chaos and disruption caused by the protest, emphasizing the inconvenience to the public and the property damage. This paints the protesters in a negative light."

He paused, eyeing the family to ensure they were following along. "Another news outlet, however, might focus on the reasons behind the protest, interviewing the protesters and highlighting their grievances. This could elicit sympathy for the protesters and their cause."

"Both news outlets report on the same event but highlight different aspects. This is biased reporting," he said, stressing the last two words. "They present facts, but in a way that leans towards a particular viewpoint. As consumers of News, it's important to recognize this."

He leaned forward, capturing their attention fully. "It's not enough to read or watch the News from just one or two sources. To get a complete and balanced view, we must seek information from various sources with different perspectives."

Vijay, Sangeeta, and Vikrant exchanged glances. This was a new way of looking at the News and understanding the information they consumed. It was a lot to take in, but they were beginning to comprehend the importance of critical thinking in navigating the information landscape.

The Kulkarni family absorbed Mr Swaminathan's words, each tip and insight etching into their minds. They were being equipped to identify Misinformation and navigate their way through the complex information landscape.

"Remember, every piece of information is like a puzzle piece," he said, his gaze holding theirs. "You need to look at it from all angles, scrutinize it before you decide where it fits in your understanding of the world."
As the conversation flowed, the Kulkarnis felt a shift. The sense of being overwhelmed slowly gave way to a sense of empowerment. They were not just passive recipients of information anymore; they were active participants in the process of knowledge creation.

As the conversation with Mr Swaminathan continued, the Kulkarnis found themselves delving deeper into the complexities of the information world. The screen that separated them seemed to dissolve, replaced by an intense atmosphere of enlightenment.

"Mr Swaminathan, how do we handle information confirming our beliefs?" Sangeeta asked, her eyebrows furrowed in thought.

"That's an excellent question, Sangeeta," Mr Swaminathan replied, nodding appreciatively. "When we come across information that aligns with our beliefs, we naturally accept it without scrutiny. But this is where the danger of confirmation bias lies."

He paused, allowing the weight of his words to sink in. "It's important to apply the same level of critical thinking and scrutiny to all information, even if it aligns with our beliefs. Always verify the source, check for supporting evidence, and consider alternative viewpoints."

Vikrant, who had been silent for a while, suddenly piped up, "But what if we end up in a situation where we cannot discern fact from fiction? What do we do then?"

Mr Swaminathan smiled, his eyes gleaming with understanding. "In such cases, it's best to consult experts in the field or turn to trusted fact-checking platforms. Remember, it's okay to not have immediate answers, and the quest for truth is a journey, not a race."

As they absorbed Mr Swaminathan's advice, each member of the Kulkarni family felt a sense of clarity. They understood their journey was about consuming information and approaching it with a critical eye, a curious mind, and an open heart.

The atmosphere in the room was charged with a newfound sense of resolve as the Kulkarnis continued their conversation with Mr Swaminathan. His wisdom was like a guiding light, illuminating the path they were about to tread.

"Mr Swaminathan," Vijay started, his voice steady. "How can we ensure that we're not contributing to the spread of misinformation ourselves?"

"Indeed, Vijay, your query strikes at the very heart of the matter," Mr Swaminathan responded. His tone was composed, but his eyes reflected the gravity of the topic. "Let's delve a little deeper into this."
He leaned back, placing his fingers together in a pyramid, "Whenever we come across a piece of information, our

initial impulse might be to share it, especially if it aligns with our beliefs or elicits a strong emotional response. But before we press that 'share' button, we must pause and ask ourselves a few questions."

"Firstly," he held up a finger, "ask yourself, 'Is this true?'

This may seem elementary, but it's surprising how often this simple step needs to be noticed.

Is the information fact-based, or is it opinion, speculation, or outright fabrication?"

"Secondly," he continued, lifting another finger, "consider the source.

Where did the information originate?

Was it a reputable news outlet, an expert, or a trusted organization? Or was it an anonymous post on a social media platform or a website known for sensationalism?"

"Thirdly," he added, his gaze firm, "question the source's reliability.

Have they been accurate in the past?

Do they have a track record of integrity and transparency? Or have they been involved in spreading Misinformation previously?"

His gaze swept across the Kulkarni family, his voice resounding in the silent room, "Each of these questions serves as a gatekeeper, preventing the spread of Misinformation. It's a process, a habit that needs to be cultivated. And remember, if you're ever in doubt, it's always better to refrain from sharing. It's our responsibility to ensure that we don't unknowingly become conduits of Misinformation."

The family absorbed his words, feeling the weight of their significance. They knew they had a role in this battle against Misinformation and were ready to play their part responsibly.

Sulochana, listening intently, spoke up, "But, sometimes, I see something interesting and want to share it with my friends. How do I know if it's true?"

Mr Swaminathan smiled warmly at her question. "Well, Sulochana, that's where your critical thinking skills come in. You can start by checking if the same News is reported by other reliable sources. And if you're still unsure, you can use online fact-checking tools or ask an adult."

The conversation flowed, with Mr Swaminathan addressing their doubts, sharing insights, and providing practical tips. As the Kulkarnis listened, they felt a sense of empowerment - they were not just passive consumers of information anymore but active seekers of truth.

Vijay turned to Mr Swaminathan, "Your advice has been invaluable, Mr Swaminathan. We've realized how important it is to be critical consumers of information. Thank you."

Mr Swaminathan's face softened, "The pleasure is mine. Remember, in this information age, being mindful and discerning is not just a skill, but a responsibility."

With these final words of wisdom, the screen faded to black. The Kulkarnis sat in silence, absorbing the profound impact of the conversation. They were no longer lost in the maze of information; they were armed with the tools and knowledge to navigate it.

CHAPTER SIX

The Awakening

The light of the following day bathed Jabalpur in a warm, golden glow. The Kulkarni household was tranquil, the lively debates and laughter of the previous day replaced by contemplative silence. Each family member was immersed in their thoughts, processing the enlightening discussion with Mr Swaminathan.

Vijay was the first to break the silence at the breakfast table. "I've been thinking about our conversation with Mr Swaminathan," he began, stirring his tea pensively. "I realized that I've been guilty of falling into the trap of misinformation more often than I'd like to admit."

Sangeeta, who was buttering toast, paused and looked at him thoughtfully. "I think we all have, Vijay. I mean, who hasn't shared a message or a post without verifying it, right?" she said, her voice softer than usual.

Vikrant, nibbling on his toast, said, "Yeah, even I've done it. Do you remember that game update rumour I told you about? I didn't verify it. I saw it on a forum, believed it, and shared it with my friends."
Sulochana, although young and not an active participant in

these conversations, was listening intently. She looked up from her cereal, her eyes round and curious. "Does that mean we shouldn't share anything at all?"

Vijay smiled at his daughter, appreciating her innocent yet insightful question. "No, dear. It means we need to be more responsible, and we need to verify the information before we share it."

The conversation flowed, and the family discussed and dissected the lessons learned. They talked about their personal experiences, the times they had been misled, and the instances they had unknowingly contributed to the spread of Misinformation.

As the day wore on, a noticeable change came over the Kulkarni household. News articles were read more discerningly, social media posts were scrutinized, and news broadcasts were questioned. It was as if they had all donned a new pair of glasses, enabling them to see the world of information in a new light.

The conversation flowed as naturally as the Ganges at dawn, weaving through the Kulkarni household. Each family member was deep in thought, digesting the newfound knowledge and its implications.

"Mr Swaminathan was right," Vijay said pensively, "We're not just consumers of information; we're creators too. We add to the information pool every time we share something and must be responsible."

This new realization was profound; it was not just about

discerning fact from fiction anymore but acknowledging the role each one played in this vast digital ecosystem.

"Mr Swaminathan's words make me think of the ripple effect," Vijay continued, his brows furrowed as he tried to put his thoughts into words. "You see when we drop a pebble into a pond, it creates ripples that spread far beyond the point of impact. Similarly, every information we share, whether true or false, creates ripples beyond our immediate network. We may not see it, but it's happening."

He paused, glancing around at his family, their faces lit by the soft glow of the dining room lights. "When we share something without verifying it, we might unintentionally spread Misinformation. It's like unknowingly dropping a pebble of falsehood into the pond of information. The ripples it creates can mislead people, cause unnecessary panic, or even harm relationships."

Vijay's analogy resonates with everyone. They understood that their actions online had far-reaching effects. Each share, like, and each comment was like a vote of confidence in a piece of information, making it more likely to be seen and believed by others.

Sangeeta added thoughtfully, "That makes sense, Vijay. And it's not just about not sharing unverified information. It's about actively promoting factual and helpful content. If we come across something that we know is true and beneficial, we should share it. That way, we're contributing positively to the information pool."

The room fell silent again as everyone contemplated their

roles as consumers and information creators. The realization was empowering and intimidating at the same time. Still, they all knew it was a responsibility they were ready to shoulder.

"I think it's about time we applied what we've learned," Sangeeta said, her voice steady and persistent. "We should start by checking the sources of information, cross-verifying the facts, and not taking everything at face value."

Vikrant looked up from his phone, usually more interested in video games than family discussions. "You know, there's a game update coming out tomorrow. Usually, I'd believe whatever the game forums say about it. But this time, I think I'll do some research independently."

Even young Sulochana seemed to grasp the gravity of their discussion. "Does that mean the cartoon character I like didn't really go to the moon?" she asked, her brows furrowing in concentration. The family laughed gently, appreciating her effort to apply their conversation to her world.

As the days passed, the Kulkarni family saw a profound shift in their interaction with information. Vijay started cross-checking political News before discussing it with friends. Sangeeta took the time to verify health tips before passing them on to her colleagues. Vikrant began scrutinizing game updates and News before sharing them with his friends.

The Kulkarni household was abuzz with change; conversations no longer centred around unverified News or the latest sensational rumour. Instead, they were full of inquiries, scepticism, and a newfound quest for truth. The family had started discussing their daily encounters with information, examining the biases, and cross-checking the sources.

One evening, the tantalizing aroma of Sangeeta's homemade biryani still hung as the Kulkarni family settled into their usual post-dinner relaxation. Vijay was perusing a book, while Vikrant and Sulochana were engrossed in their respective devices. Sangeeta, cradling a cup of her favourite green tea, was scrolling through her social media feed.

Suddenly, she paused, her eyebrows furrowing at a post that caught her eye. "Listen to this," she said, breaking the comfortable silence. "It says here that a certain herb can prevent heart attacks, and it's been shared by a wellness page I follow." She held out her phone to the family, the light from the screen illuminating her worried expression.

Vikrant, who had been training his scepticism muscle over the past few weeks, took the phone from his mother. He skimmed the post, his eyes narrowing in suspicion. "Mom, just because this information comes from a wellness page doesn't mean it's accurate or complete," he warned, echoing Mr Swaminathan's words from their previous conversation.

Vijay put down his book, interested. "Well, it might not be entirely false. Many herbs have medicinal properties," he said, stroking his chin.

"But Dad," Sulochana chimed in, her 10-year-old mind

sharp as a tack, "just because some herbs are good doesn't mean all herbs can prevent heart attacks, right?"

Vikrant nodded, "Exactly, Sulochana. We need to verify this, and let's look up some medical journals or trusted health websites." He opened a new tab in his browser, his fingers typing in the herb's name.

As the Kulkarni family huddled around the computer, their faces lit by the soft glow of the screen, they realized they were not just a family enjoying their evening but a team, a unit fighting the wave of Misinformation together. And in that moment, they felt a strange sense of empowerment. They were taking control of the information they consumed, becoming passive receivers and active seekers of truth.

The family spent the next half an hour researching the claim. They discovered that while the herb had some heart-healthy properties, it was no magic bullet for preventing heart attacks. The wellness page had twisted the facts to make a sensational claim.

Vijay sighed, "Imagine how many people might have believed this and shared it. This is precisely why we need to be cautious."

One late evening, as the television played in the background, Vijay's phone buzzed with a new message. It was from Sameer, his old friend, now a seasoned news reporter in the bustling city of New Delhi. The announcement was terse but impactful: "Major political rally in Jabalpur suspected to cause a surge in virus cases."

Vijay stared at the message, instantly recalling Kapil's caution about potential biases in media reporting. He remembered Kapil's words, "News is like a multi-faceted gem. Every facet reflects a different angle of the story, each coloured by its own biases."

With this in mind, Vijay decided to dig deeper. He opened his laptop and began navigating various news portals, his fingers flying over the keys as he sifted through articles, videos, and social media posts.
Some news outlets condemned the political rally, blaming the virus surge squarely on the event. But others painted a different picture, citing general laxity in following safety protocols across the city as the leading cause.

Vijay leaned back in his chair, rubbing his temples as he processed the information. He realized the reality was more complex than it initially seemed. With its massive crowd, the political rally was undoubtedly a contributing factor. But it was just one piece of a giant puzzle. The virus didn't discriminate between a political rally, a crowded market, or a packed bus. The lapse in safety protocols was widespread, seeping into every corner of the city.

Turning his gaze towards the window, Vijay could see the city lights twinkling in the distance. He felt a strange mix of relief and worry. Relief because he had seen through the veil of bias, fear because he realized how easy it was to be swept away by a tide of Misinformation.

Over breakfast, he shared his findings with his family the following day. "It's like peeling an onion," he explained,

"There are many layers to the truth. It's not black and white but a spectrum of greys. And it's our responsibility to navigate through it."

The Kulkarni household was transforming, and so were its members. Each day was a step towards becoming consumers and responsible information creators. As they navigated this path, they were awakening to the reality of the world around them and sparking a change within themselves that they hoped would ripple into their community. The journey was far from over, but the family felt prepared and motivated to face the challenges ahead in the information jungle.

CHAPTER SEVEN

The Final Test

In the quiet early hours of a Tuesday, the sun painted streaks of pink and orange across the sky over Jabalpur. The Kulkarni household, though, was buzzing with activity. The aroma of fresh coffee wafted through the house, mingling with the smell of crispy toast.

Vijay was scanning the morning newspaper, his eyes skimming through the local news section. Sangeeta was packing lunch for Vikrant, who was engrossed in his latest gaming conquest. Sulochana, the youngest Kulkarni, meticulously arranged her school bag, her brows furrowed in concentration.

Suddenly, the peace was shattered by the jarring ring of Vijay's phone. It was Sameer, his friend and a local news reporter. Sameer sounded troubled, his voice carrying an urgency that sent a chill down Vijay's spine. "Vijay, there's a rumour going around town that a group of extremists is planning a strike at the city centre today. It's causing panic. But my sources say it might be a hoax. I thought you could help verify."

The News was like a thunderbolt. The family looked at each other, their faces reflecting the same shock and determination. This was the moment of their final test.

"Okay, we'll do what we can to help," Vijay responded, his voice steady despite the racing heartbeat.
The Kulkarnis had transformed into a fact-checking command centre at the heart of their living room. Sulochana's fingers moved fiercely over her tablet, her brows furrowed in concentration as she combed through local news sites. She scrutinized each headline, her experienced eyes searching for any sign of the rumoured attack. She navigated the sea of information with newfound agility, her previous hesitation replaced by a confident determination.

In another corner, Vikrant was engrossed in a world of hashtags and trending topics. He scrolled through various social media platforms, his eyes darting across his phone screen, decoding the digital chatter. He was trying to spot any signs of panic or confirmation of the rumoured attack. His fingers danced on the screen, opening links, verifying sources, and cross-referencing information, all while keeping an eye on the growing anxiety in the online community.

With her innate ability to remain calm in a crisis, Sangeeta chose a different approach. She picked up her phone and started contacting her friends in the local community. She knew that people on the ground often had the most accurate information in times of uncertainty. Her voice was steady, her questions clear and concise. She listened attentively to their responses, piecing together a picture of the ground reality from their perspectives.

Each of them worked independently, but their actions had an underlying synchronicity. They were united by a common purpose, a shared responsibility to uncover the truth and prevent the spread of panic and Misinformation. Their home, usually a haven of warmth and laughter, had momentarily transformed into a hub of intense focus and unwavering resolve.

As the day wore on, their efforts began bearing fruit. The more they delved, the more they realized that the rumour was indeed baseless, a result of an offhand remark taken out of context and blown out of proportion.

As they sat around the dining table, their dinner plates forgotten, the Kulkarnis looked at each other.
"This is exactly what Mr Swaminathan was talking about, right?" Sulochana's voice broke the silence. "The rumour is creating fear, and fear spreads faster than anything."

Vijay nodded, his mind working furiously. "Indeed, Sulochana. But remember, we have learned how to deal with this, and we need to verify this information before reacting."

Vikrant's eyes, usually sparkling with mischief, were now serious as he looked up from his phone. His fingers, which were dancing across the screen just moments ago, were now still. The light from the screen illuminated his face, casting a sombre shadow over his usually jovial expression.
"The digital landscape is buzzing with chatter about the rumoured attack," he began, his voice echoing the gravity of his expression.

He carried on with his exposition, his voice steady and calm despite the severity of the situation, "I've plunged into the extensive recesses of the leading social media platforms, from Facebook and Twitter to Instagram and TikTok. I've followed the winding trails of the trending hashtags, their footprints treading across the virtual landscape, and I've examined an overwhelming number of posts, each adding fuel to the growing fire of the rumour."

Vikrant's hands moved animatedly, mirroring the fervour of his words, "The rumour is omnipresent, propagating at an alarming speed. It's like a wildfire, unchecked and out of control, consuming logic and reasoning in its path."

Then, he paused, his gaze sweeping across each family member, ensuring he had their undivided attention. The silence in the room was almost tangible, as if even the air held its breath, waiting for his following words.

"But here's the crux of the matter," he resumed, his tone serious, every word carefully weighed, "None of these posts, none of these wildfire-like rumours, have any credible sources. It's all hearsay. One person whispers it to the next, and the next, and so on. It's like a gigantic game of Chinese whispers, the initial message distorted beyond recognition."

He sighed, a hint of frustration creeping into his voice, "No one is pausing to question the claim's authenticity. No one is taking the initiative to verify the information. It's just mindless propagation. And that's how Misinformation spreads, unchecked and unchallenged."

His revelation cast a sobering light on the situation, highlighting the intricacies of the misinformation web they were ensnared in. It was a powerful reminder of their mission and the challenges ahead.

The room fell silent as his words sunk in. Then, he concluded with a sense of certainty in his voice, "This, my friends, seems like a classic case of Misinformation. It has all the hallmarks - the rapid spread, the absence of credible sources, and the sense of urgency it creates. This is exactly what Kapil and Mr Swaminathan warned us about."

As he finished, he looked around the room, his gaze meeting the thoughtful faces of his family. They had been tested, and they had risen to the challenge. The lessons they had learned were now being put into practice, and they were standing their ground against the wave of Misinformation.

Sangeeta said, "I spoke to friends who live near the city centre. They've seen nothing out of the ordinary today."

Vijay looked at his family, pride welling up in his chest. "Good job, everyone. Let's not stop here. We should inform Sameer about what we found, and he can help quell the panic with the right information."

They spent the next hour reaching out to their respective networks, spreading the word about the baseless rumour. With every message they sent, they felt a sense of accomplishment. They were not just passive information consumers anymore but active participants in the fight against Misinformation.

Later, as they finally sat down to eat, there was a sense of camaraderie and satisfaction. They had faced a challenging situation, and they had navigated it well. They had applied their newly acquired knowledge about Misinformation and its pitfalls and emerged victorious.

And so, when Sameer called later that night to thank them and share that the panic had been mainly diffused, they couldn't help but feel a sense of accomplishment. They had made a difference, however slight, in their community.

"Is this how it's going to be from now on?" Kapil asked, his voice echoing through the video call. There was a distinct note of worry in his voice. His question hung in the air, making everyone at the dinner table stop and think.

Vijay, looking thoughtful, was the first to respond. "It's not going to be easy, Kapil. But remember, we have the tools to tackle this. We've learned to question, to verify, to think critically."

Sulochana added, "And we've seen how Misinformation can impact us directly. We can't afford to let our guard down, not when it's about our family, friends, and community."

Sangeeta, who had been silently listening, suddenly spoke up. "This is our responsibility. We're not just passive receivers of information. We're active participants in this ecosystem. And we can make a difference."

Vikrant nodded in agreement. "Exactly, Mom. And it's not

just us. If we can learn to handle Misinformation, so can others, and we should help our friends and community understand this."

The conversation continued late into the night, with each family member sharing their thoughts and ideas. Despite the situation's intensity, there was an undercurrent of hope and determination. They had faced their first real test since understanding the dangers of Misinformation, and they had emerged more assertive and more resolved.

As they finally bid each other goodnight, they knew their journey was far from over. They had challenges to face and battles to fight. But they were ready. Armed with knowledge, guided by the light of truth, the Kulkarnis were prepared to navigate the maze of Misinformation.

And so, when they woke up the next day to a message from Sameer thanking them for their help and informing them that the panic had been successfully diffused, they couldn't help but feel a sense of pride and accomplishment.

They had passed their final test and made a difference in their community. And as they embarked on a new day, they knew this was just the beginning of their journey in the battle against Misinformation.

Conclusion

And so, the Kulkarni family emerged from the misinformation maze, forever changed by their journey. Their experience is not just a tale unique to them but a mirror held up to every family and individual in today's digital age. It was a journey that challenged traditions, toppled misconceptions, and carved new paths of understanding. It was a journey that empowered them to distinguish fact from fiction, steering clear of the pitfalls of Misinformation.

When they began, the Kulkarni family were unsuspecting information consumers, unaware of the dangers lurking in the vast digital landscape. But as they navigated the maze, they started to question, research, and discern. They learned about cognitive biases, the echo chamber effect, the importance of seeking credible sources, and the pitfalls of biased reporting. They came face-to-face with the reality that Misinformation was not a nebulous concept but a natural force that could stir chaos, propagate fear, and cause real-world harm.

Above all, they learned that they had the power to counter it.

Vijay, the patriarch, discovered the importance of setting aside his political inclinations when interpreting News. Sangeeta, the wellness enthusiast, recognized the need to cross-check information before accepting it as truth. Kapil, the digital native, acknowledged his role in preventing the spread of Misinformation within his online community.

And young Sulochana, just 10 years old, became aware of the power of technology and its potential dangers, demonstrating an understanding beyond her years.

They charted a new course of responsible information consumption and dissemination as a unit, leading them out of the misinformation maze.

The Kulkarni family's journey is a lesson for us all. It underscores that we are not mere spectators but active participants in today's digital world. Every tweet we send, every post we approve, and every news item we forward have the potential to shape perceptions, influence beliefs, and shift realities. We are responsible for ensuring the information we propagate is accurate, unbiased, and verified.

As we close this chapter on the Kulkarni family, let's absorb the lessons they've imparted. Let's strive to be responsible digital citizens, questioning more, accepting less, and relentlessly seeking the truth.
Because navigating the misinformation maze is not just a one-time journey; it's an ongoing commitment to truth in our digital lives.

As the story of the Kulkarni family continues to unfold, it is clear that their experience with the labyrinth of Misinformation was not a mere incident but a transformational journey that resonates with every digital citizen of the world.

After this transformative journey, the Kulkarni family changed their day-to-day lives. Evenings that were once filled with the drone of the television news were now replaced with engaging conversations, discussions, and debates. Dinners became an occasion for sharing and discussing the day's News and information, not just consuming it. The family was no longer a passive consumer of information; they had become active participants, questioning, verifying, and discussing everything they encountered.

Vijay, who used to spend his evenings voraciously reading news articles online, now devoted time to cross-checking information, referring to multiple sources, and drawing his own conclusions. Sangeeta, the health enthusiast, no longer trusted every health tip she received on her social media platforms. Instead, she researched, questioned, and verified the information before sharing it with her friends and family.

Vikrant, already an active netizen, became a digital soldier, fighting the good fight against Misinformation within his online communities. He started a blog to share his learnings, helping others navigate the digital space responsibly.

And young Sulochana, the vibrant and curious 10-year-old, was no longer the little girl who believed in every story she heard. She had become a young information warrior, intuitively questioning every information she received, a testament that it's always early enough to start.

The Kulkarni family's transformation wasn't just limited to their home. It reverberated through their friends, their community, and their city. They advocated for responsible information sharing, leading by example, and inspiring others to do the same.

The Misinformation Maze is not just a tale of a family's journey. It is a call to action. It's a reminder that we are all digital citizens in an increasingly connected world. Every piece of information we share, every post we like, and every story we forward has a consequence.

Let's not wait for a crisis to jolt us into awareness. Let's begin our journey through the maze today. The Kulkarni family found their way out; so can we. As we close this book, let's carry its lessons forward and commit to being responsible digital citizens.

The digital world is vast and the maze of misinformation complex, but armed with the right tools and awareness, we can navigate it successfully. Let's pledge to do so for ourselves, our families, and our global community. Because, in the end, the truth is not just out there. It's in our hands.

Afterword

I hope you have found "The Misinformation Maze: A Tale of Family, Facts, and Fiction" enlightening as we reach the end of the book. In this digital era, we have access to an abundance of information. Still, unfortunately, we also can spread false information at an alarming rate. This fictional story highlights a genuine and pressing issue that is prevalent in our society - the subject of Misinformation.

The Kulkarni family's story represents the struggle of ordinary people against this global challenge. Each character embodies someone we know, from the young Sulochana to Vijay, Sangeeta, and Kapil. They serve as a reminder that no one is immune to Misinformation, but everyone can do something about it.

The Kulkarnis' transformation from passive consumers to responsible information creators is a journey we should all take. This story is not only about the problem, but it also provides a solution. It demonstrates that we hold the antidote to Misinformation through questioning, scepticism, and verification before sharing.

As you read about the Kulkarnis, I hope you reflected on your information consumption and sharing habits. The characters' actions provide valuable lessons for navigating the digital information space.

Writing this book has reinforced my belief in the power of awareness and knowledge, and I hope it has done the same for you. As we navigate the vast digital landscape, let us do so with responsibility and discernment, knowing that our actions can contribute to the problem or the solution.

"The Misinformation Maze" is not just a story. It is a call to action, urging us to be responsible citizens of the digital world. Let's carry the lessons we've learned into our lives and turn the tide against Misinformation. We all have a role to play in the battle for truth. Thank you for joining me on this journey.

9 798890 660497

Printed by Libri Plureos GmbH in Hamburg, Germany